Jude Rogers and Alex Farebrother-Naylor

Pop! ISBN 978-0-9930773-3-3
Fisherton Press Ltd

www.fishertonpress.co.uk

First published in 2016 in the United Kingdom

Text © Jude Rogers 2016
Illustrations © Alex Farebrother-Naylor 2016

ISBN 978-0-9930773-3-3
A CIP catalogue record for this book is available from the British Library

No part of this book shall be reproduced or transmitted in any form or by any means, electronic or mechanical, including photocopying, recording, or by any information retrieval system, without the prior permission of the publisher.

The right of Jude Rogers to be identified as the author of this work has been asserted by her in accordance with the Copyrights, Designs and Patents Act, 1988.

The right of Alex Farebrother-Naylor to be identified as the illustrator of this work has been asserted by her in accordance with the Copyrights, Designs and Patents Act, 1988.

JR - For Dan, Evan, Bananarama and Kraftwerk x

AF-N - For Helen, Frieda, Ed, Kate Bush and the Pet Shop Boys x

A note for adults

This book is intended as a tribute to everyone who has ever made, produced or listened to pop music. The people in this book represent the genres, artists and types of artist that we feel help tell the story of pop music. As such many of the images depict everyday fans dressing up as their heroes and copying their styles and accessories, and are not intended to suggest that any artists have endorsed this book or its contents.

Since the very first people existed,
we have made music.

But something special happened in the 1950s.

Pop music
was invented.

Older people were suspicious about this ...

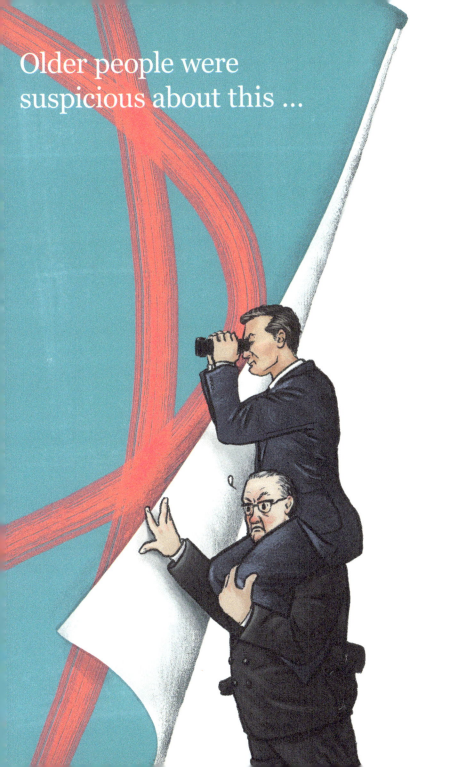

... which made young people like it even more.

Pop music is about telling stories.

Stories about loving people with all your heart.

Stories about when you feel happy or sad.

Stories of adventures you've had.

Sometimes it's about telling people in charge that you don't like what they're doing.

... small sounds and big noisy noises.

Shy people, loud people, serious people, silly people.

Some of them like jumping.
Some of them like screaming.

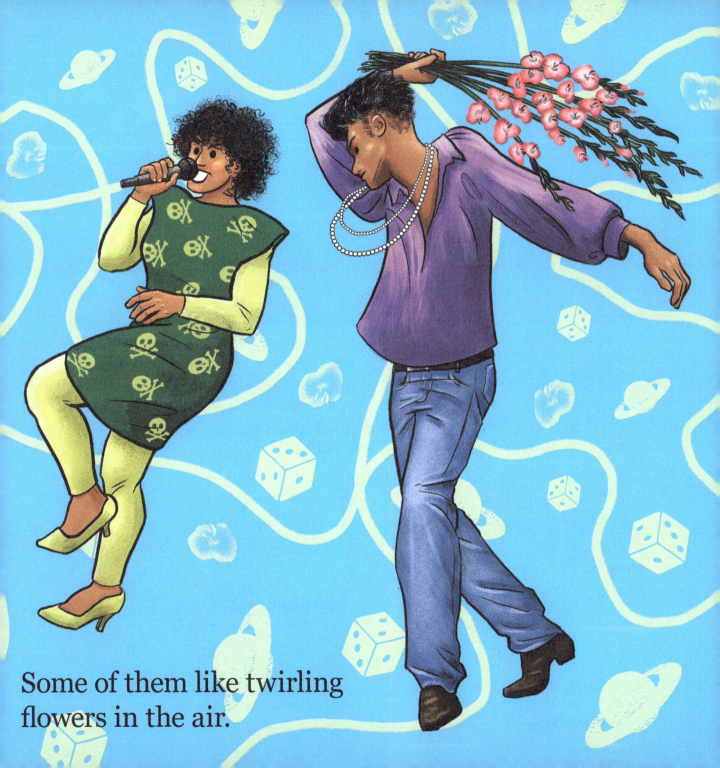
Some of them like twirling flowers in the air.

Pop music lets you be whoever you want to be.

Some people like to use instruments.

Some people make music alone and some make music with others.

Just as some people like to listen to music alone and some like to listen with others.

Pop music can be a way to connect with people when you can't find the right words, or don't speak the same language.

And when people like the same music, there can be a special bond between them.

It is hard to know what pop music will do next.

Each generation makes it their own.

If you enjoyed this book...

Tell:
- your local librarian
- your teacher
- your friends
- your local bookshop

Write:
- to us general@fishertonpress.co.uk
- blog about it
- on social media #FishertonPress
- review it online

Buy:
- a copy for a friend
- birthday presents
- other Fisherton books
- and donate a book via our website

www.fishertonpress.co.uk

Maroon Bells, USA

Great Barrier Reef, Australia

Moraine Lake, Canada

Lake Bled, Slovenia

Bora Bora, French Polynesia

Sossusvlei, Namibia

Salar de Uyuni, Bolivia

Antelope Canyon, Arizona

Arashiyama Bamboo Grove, Japan

Halong Bay, Vietnam

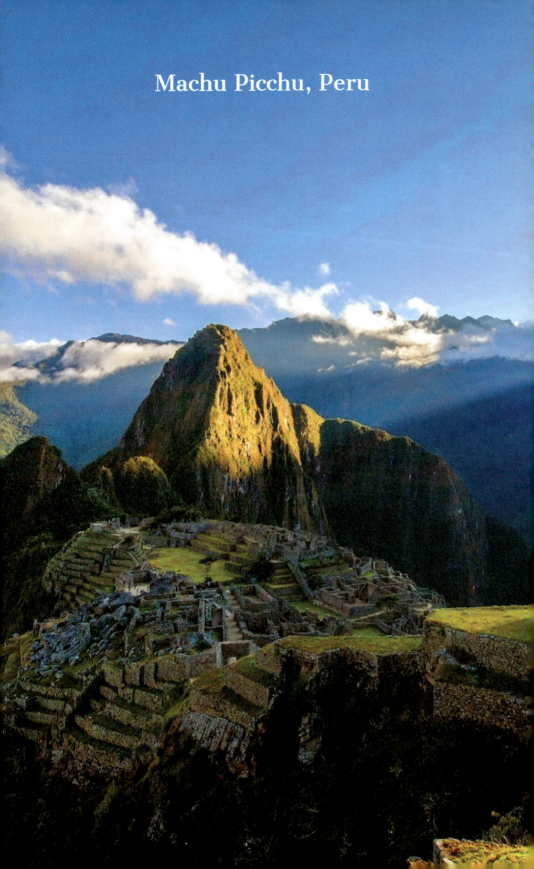
Machu Picchu, Peru

Raja Ampat Islands, Indonesia

Torres del Paine, National Park, Chile

Zakynthos, Greece

Bagan, Myanmar

Reine, Norway

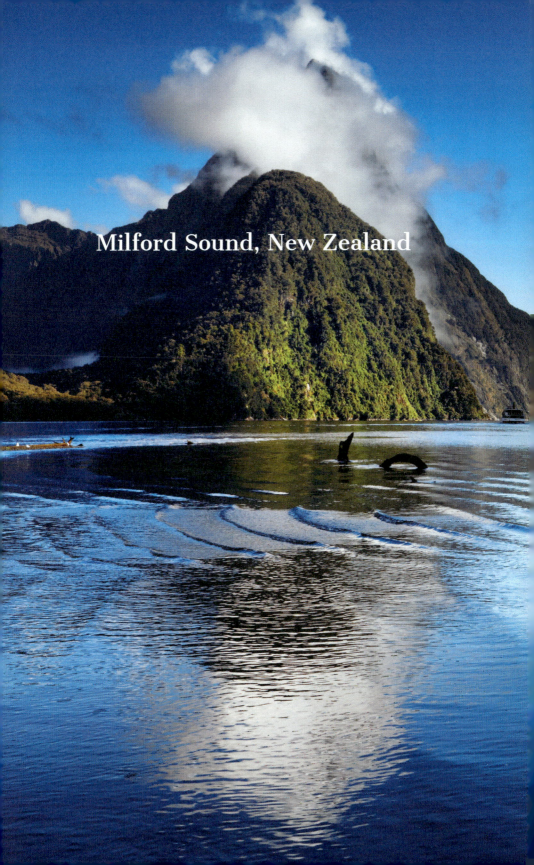

Twelve Apostles, Australia

Neuschwanstein Castle, Germany

Sa Pa, Vietname

Printed in Great Britain
by Amazon